AF469287

ALL THIS

Contents

SLAYER

FOREWORD

ALL THIS MAYHEM is a major exhibition of newly commissioned and recent work by internationally renowned, San Francisco-based artist Ben Venom that exemplifies his interest in the DIY aspect of punk culture combined with the tradition of quilting.

The exhibition features large-scale textile pieces and customised jean jackets. Venom creates stunning, expansive patchwork designs that often incorporate skulls, tigers and heavy metal lyrics with his practice framed within wider counterculture contexts, and the legacy of post-war American art and craft.

Venom's early influences come from the street – punk rock, heavy metal, and the skateboard community, leading the artist to apply his more recent work in many directions from major museum exhibitions to commercially-driven branded commissions. At the heart of Venom's work is his use of re-purposed materials to create textile-based pieces, contrasting the often menacing and iconic counterculture components of gangs, punk/metal music and the occult with the comforts of domesticity.

The reclaimed fabrics that are used in Venom's work contain a multitude of personal histories, some donated by music fans and friends, with everyone's unexplained stain, tear, or rip included. These salvaged pieces are sewn into a larger narrative and become a part of a collective history within the work. The fragility of the materials and their assaulting imagery are brought together in the form of a functional piece of art.

Traditional quilting is often a communal activity, made in quilting circles. It offers rich associations of family, tradition, the domestic, handmade, recycled and embodies an emotional connection between the quilter and their relationship to the community. Historically as quilts began to move off the bed and onto the wall, from the 1960's onwards, it was inevitable that they began to be seen in relationship to painting and drawing, more commonly associated with 'male dominated' materials and art forms. In relation to Venom's work we see commonplace materials and techniques that intermingle fine art and craft, dispelling gender stereotypes of contemporary quilting practice and expressing a fresh and irreverent sense of masculinity. Whilst Venom

left: *See You on the Other Side*, Hand-made quilt with recycled fabric, 155" x 175" (394 x 445cm), 2011

makes his work independently in his studio, rather than with a quilting circle, his 'family' is drawn from a wider cultural community of makers/creatives that seek to inform his work, whether they be musicians, skateboarders or artists.

The collision of traditional quilting techniques with elements tied to the fringes of society re-contextualises both the perceptions of quilting as an art form and the use of counterculture motifs in art.

The exhibition has been produced by Midlands Arts Centre in partnership with Home of Metal. This is part of a region-wide season, conceived and produced by Capsule, dedicated to the phenomena of heavy metal music and the fans and aficionados devoted to the music that was born in and around Birmingham. It is music that turned up the volume, down-tuned the guitars, and introduced a new meaning to the word 'heavy'. Underpinning the season is a seminal exhibition *Black Sabbath – 50 Years* presented at Birmingham Museum and Art Gallery, alongside a wider season of dynamic events and exhibitions that unite music, social history, art and fan cultures to produce a new perspective on metal culture.

We must thank Lindsay Bishop and Laura L. Camerlengo for their insightful catalogue essays which offer such celebratory considerations on the work, and also to Jessica Litherland, MAC's Visual Arts Producer for shaping the exhibition so skilfully. Financial support comes from Arts Council England, The Postcode Culture Trust and The Roughley Trust for whom we are eternally grateful.

Above all, we are extremely grateful to Ben Venom. He is a remarkable artist and our admiration for his beautiful work could not be more heartfelt.

Deborah Kermode
Chief Executive and Artistic Director, MAC

The Devil Inside Me,
Custom Fabricated Jacket,
Collaboration with Truth Never Told,
20" x 25" (51 x 63.5cm), 2018

The Devil Inside Me, (back view and detail)

N
F

Iron Fist,
hand-made quilt with recycled fabric
95" x 60" (241 x152.5cm), 2017

DIRTY
DEEDS
DONE
DIRT
CHEAP
ELECTRIC FUNERAL
LUSTY LADY

MISTER MAYHEM

IN JUST OVER A DECADE, San Francisco–based artist Ben Venom has achieved international renown for his unparalleled ability to combine the ideas and aesthetics of what he calls the 'fringes of society'[1] with the centuries-old tradition of quilting. His work draws upon many visual codes simultaneously: those of the occult, motorcycle clubs, tattoo culture, punk rock, and heavy metal, among other countercultural influences, as well as the complex symbolism of quilts. By this practice, Venom has forged a new creative vision that concurrently inhabits and blurs the boundaries of artistic expression and domestic production, individual memory and collective identity, and male and female gender binaries. As Venom himself describes, "In one word, my work can be described as a collision."[2]

Throughout their history, quilts have served as signifiers of hearth, home, and ancestral heritage; as indicators of familial relationships and markers of domestic production; and as manifestations of artistry. The practice of quilting – or sewing together two or more layers of fabric to form a dense textile – has thrived in the United States since colonial times, when single pieces of cloth and, later, fragments of new and salvaged clothing and textiles were stitched together to form warm barriers against a harsh climate. Venom first became interested in quilts in 2006 as a graduate student at the San Francisco Art Institute. The artist, who had previously worked in painting and printmaking, visited the de Young museum in San Francisco's Golden Gate Park, where he saw *The Quilts of Gee's Bend* (July 16, 2006–January 1, 2007), an exhibition of quilts made by four generations of African American women from a remote area of Alabama. Not only did the bold, improvisational compositions of the quilts appeal to Venom's artistic sensibilities, but their origins in the American South left the Charleston, South Carolina-born artist with an acute feeling of homesickness. Venom was also struck by the Gee's Bend quilters' reuse of fabric scraps and salvaged work clothes, which recalled his experiences of do-it-yourself creation in the South. As a child, "My mom had a sewing machine, and my father is a very good handyman who was always fixing stuff around the house."[3]

Venom grew up outside of Atlanta in Cobb County, Georgia, a middle-class community known for its political and social conservatism. He compares his high school

left and overleaf: *Monument to Thieves*, Hand-made quilt with recycled fabric, 95" x 67" (241 x 170cm), 2016

DEEDS
DIRT
LUSTY LADY

DIRTY
IRON M
MEGA
DONE
ELECTRIC
FUNERAL

experiences to Francis Ford Coppola's 1983 coming-of-age film, *The Outsiders*: "In a graduating class of a few hundred students, there was a strong divide between the jocks and the punks,"[4] he says. As a teenager, Venom immersed himself in Atlanta's punk scene. This was not only where he earned his 'Venom' moniker – his given name is Ben Baumgartner – but where his interest in do-it-yourself artistry was sparked:

"[The scene] entailed mostly going to house shows in people's basements, garages, driveways, backyards. The bands would screen-print patches, T-shirts, etc. to make gas money to make it to their next show. There was a really strong do-it-yourself work ethic that kind of carried out through the scene, and I totally took that into adulthood."[5]

Within the Gee's Bend quilts, Venom observed old denim jeans, T-shirts, and blankets that had been sourced from the local community; once worn, these materials were crafted into functional quilts that would also be used by community members. "Everyone's personal memories – unexplained stain, tear, or rip – can then live on in a second life in the form of something entirely different from its initial purpose," says Venom. "It was this lifecycle of fabric that... I was directly interested in and inspired by."[6]

Quilt making has a long history of community participation; over the centuries, innumerable groups of quilters have gathered to work on individual or communal quilting projects. In his own artistic practice, Venom too incorporates the communities with which he associates. Although he sews alone, his textiles are often formed from threadbare band tees, ripped jeans, old leather jackets, and other worn garments donated by friends, which he pieces together to form new works that evoke the aesthetics, insignias, and mantras of the punk and heavy metal communities. Many are odes to Black Sabbath, "an all-time favorite band"[7] of Venom's; as one example, the title of Sabbath's apocalyptic ode 'Electric Funeral,' from their second studio album, *Paranoid*, is inscribed on a pedestal bearing a growling fluorescent-fabric lion on Venom's oversized *Monument to Thieves* quilt.

The subversion of stereotypical gender norms that Venom represents as a male quilter in a traditionally female sphere is further reinforced by his evoking the nonconforming masculinity sometimes found in the heavy metal and hard rock communities, especially among performers. Along with others, Black Sabbath, American heavy metal bands Quiet Riot and Twisted Sister, and later rock act Cinderella feminised their appearances – with long hair, dramatic makeup, and body-conscious clothing – to assert their virility. On the shoulder of a custom fabricated jacket made in collaboration with the Los Angeles collective Truth Never Told, Sabbath vocalist Ozzy Osbourne appears with full hair, thick eyeliner, and fangs bared.

left: *King of Kings*, hand-made quilt with recycled fabric, 75" x 75" (190 x 190cm), 2012

As often found in both the music and textile histories his art draws upon, many of the motifs and lyrics found in Venom's quilts are tied to Venom's intimate, personal memories. 'Never Say Die!,' which appears prominently on the back of a jacket of pieced python print and denim, seemingly adopts the title of Sabbath's eighth studio album, but the phrase also recalls the tagline of Richard Donner's enduring adventure tale *The Goonies* (1985), which Venom first saw as a child. Rendered in Gothic script and dominating a quilt made from diamond-shaped pieces of old jeans, 'No More Tears' evokes Ozzy Osbourne's song of the same name but also reminds Venom of the slogan for Johnson's Baby Shampoo, which his mother would use to wash his hair as a child. These recollections – of childhood, home, and family life – also prove tangible links to the domestic origins and inherent functionality of quilts. As Venom explains, "At the end of the day, my art still serves a distinct purpose in the world. If hell freezes over, you can keep warm with one of my quilts."[8]

Laura L. Camerlenso
Costume and Textiles Curator

NOTES:

1 Ben Venom, interview with author, March 12, 2019.

2 Ibid.

3 Kristin Farr, 'Ben Venom: Thrill of It All,' *Juxtapoz* (July 2015): 65.

4 Ben Venom, interview with author, March 12, 2019.

5 KQED Art School, 'Episode 59: Ben Venom is a Punk Rock Quilter: What's Your Style?,' PBS video, 2:42, March 14, 2015, https://www.pbs.org/video/art-school-ben-venom-punk-rock-quilter-whats-your-style/.

6 Ibid.

7 Ben Venom, interview with author, March 12, 2019.

8 Ben Venom, interview with author, March 12, 2019.

right: *No More Tears*,
hand-made quilt with recycled fabric,
75" x 79" (190 x 200cm), 2013

NO
MORE
TEARS

Don't Tread On Me!,
hand-made quilt with recycled fabric,
155" x 87" (394 x 221cm), 2015

HARLEY-DAVIDSON
HARLEY-DAVIDSON
AWFUL
AWFUL
DON'T TREAD ON ME!

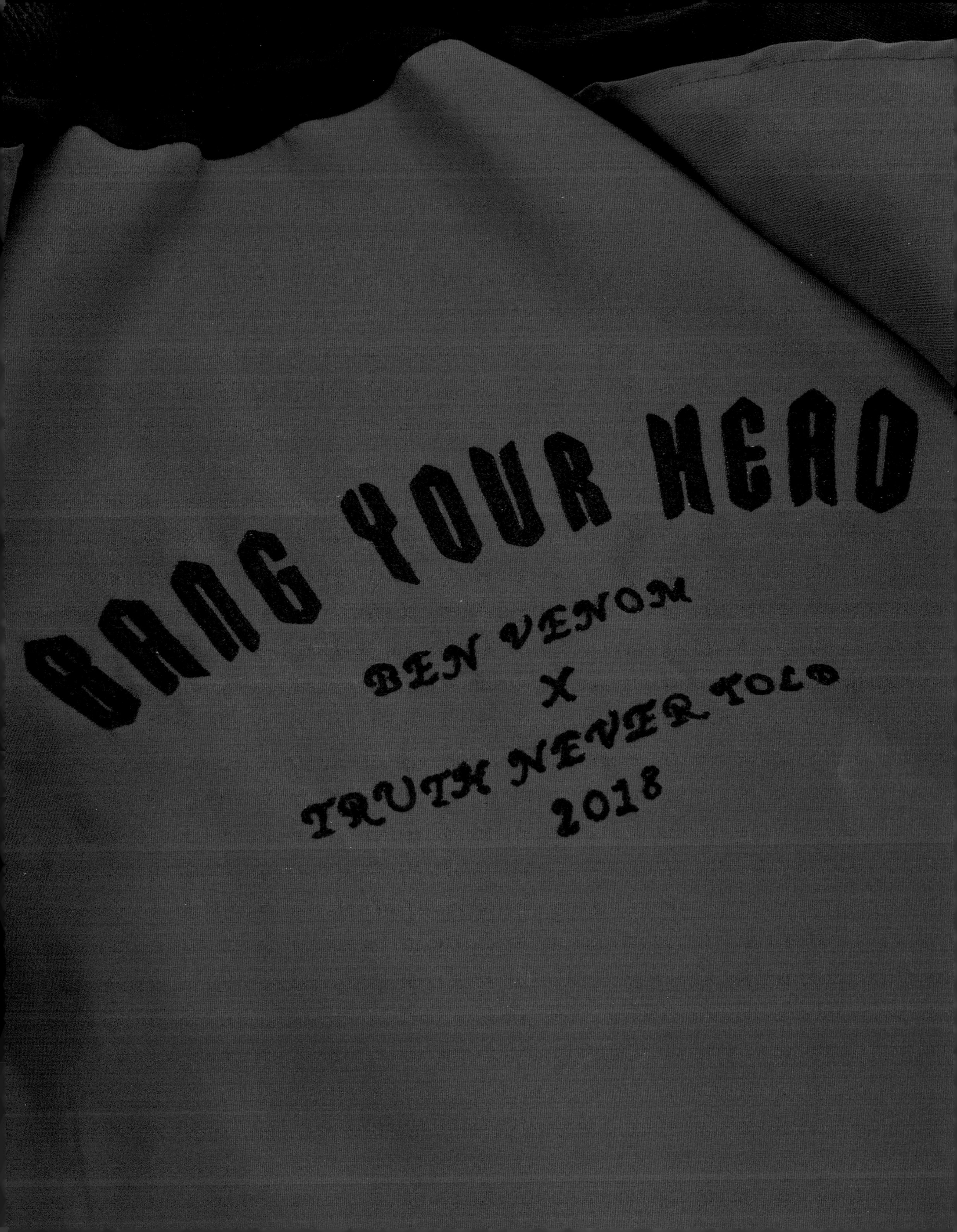

BANG YOUR HEAD

BEN VENOM
X
TRUTH NEVER TOLD
2018

Ben Venom
TRUTH NEVER TOLD

Never
say
Die!

Never Say Die!,
Custom Fabricated Jacket,
Collaboration with Truth Never Told,
20" x 25" (51 x 63.5cm), 2018

Bang Your Head
Custom Fabricated Jacket
Collaboration with Truth Never Told
20" x 25" (51 x 63.5cm), 2018

COLLISION OF COMMUNITY

MUSIC HAS, FOR SOME TIME, been considered an aural experience. It makes sense, we *listen* to music therefore it is an *aural* art form. Water is wet. Yes, yes?... no.

Bear with me.

Sitting alone at my favourite table in the corner of a London metal bar, surrounded by strangers and yet totally at home, it occurs to me that this idea of music as something just to listen to is lunacy – as far as heavy metal is concerned anyway.

Metal, for those fortunate enough to find themselves possessed by this beast, is far from just an aural experience. It clothes us, decorates our houses, our bodies, our cars, takes us away on damp camping weekends, bonds us with new friends for life and introduces us to an extended global family. For the brave it is the soundtrack to some of our most intimate interactions and thanks in part to the internet it now feeds us too.[1]

In short, metal = community

Community

The significance in Ben Venom's quilts lies in that they represent a materialisation of metal as greater than the extraordinarily absurd spectacle most associate it with. In his own words he creates a deliberate *collision* of the darker aesthetics of heavy metal with the domesticity of quilt making. This speaks directly to the everyday nature of heavy metal as a community that not only involves dedicated hours spent at home sewing patches onto battle vests, but time and dedication are also committed to incorporating metal into the home, the office, anywhere. The impact of this music is such that there is a desire to become completely immersed: metal is lived and breathed both publicly and privately throughout people's lives. The music is certainly the priority but an understanding of the language of metal aesthetics lets people easily identify and relate to each other in person. A group of metal heads wearing a range of band shirts may look the same to some, but it's a guarantee that a Lamb of God devotee can identify a likeminded soul at thirty paces with ease.

"Quilting has a long history of being a community based process where everyone comes together to work on the quilt. Since, I do all the work entirely myself...my community is made of people I know in bands that have donated shirts, patches etc.

for me to use. The majority of my work uses recycled or donated material that becomes the foundation of the designs." BV

Style

It should also be noted that metal's dark aesthetics are not a mindless middle finger to those who find the music and the imagery abhorrent. Those who wear their metal patches and T-shirts with pride will be all too familiar with the scoff: "why do they all look alike if they are trying to be so *individual?*". The reason these shirts are worn is not an attempt to be unique, instead they represent a meaningful connection to music that continues to resonate with them throughout their lives. Inexplicable as it may seem to outsiders, this fierce racket and nefarious imagery are positively appetising to us inside those shadowy bars yelling and struggling to hear one another over the music because to turn it down… well that is just not an option.

"Style for me is… consciously formed over time, you get influenced by things every day and you catalogue that as you grow as an artist and as a person." BV

Collision

Venom's work is both an extension and a representation of the relationship that connects materials, music and community.

From his first piece which was created using his personal T-shirt collection, each subsequent quilt contains a collection of used and damaged fabrics, rife with the personal histories of the previous occupiers. It is essential that these materials possess their own experiences, and Venom has taken on the task for breathing new life into these fabrics, giving them a second chance whilst celebrating their original purpose.

"…everyone's unexplained stain, tear, or rip is included. These salvaged pieces are sewn into a larger narrative and become a part of a collective history within the work." BV

Indeed, one of the unifying habits of this global community is a reverence for collected band T-shirts. They are bought at meaningful performances and worn for years. Even when they become unwearable the fabric is kept; to part from this material would be like denying an indispensable part of our personal history. These T-shirts in a sense have a life of their own.

"This first quilt I made contained my collection of Heavy Metal band shirts. For years I had amassed a large pile of torn up and threadbare band shirts that I could never throw away. It's not cool when your Slayer shirt turns to mesh. Ha!" BV

pages 30, right and 35: *Black Sabbath F.C.*, Custom Fabricated Jacket
Collaboration with Truth Never Told, 20" x 25" (51 x 63.5cm), 2019

AVFC
32Red
Sabbath
hell

"I can't throw them away. The first T-shirt I bought was the first time I went to a festival and I've certainly still got it… I don't think I'll ever throw it away, even though the sleeves came off, but I won't throw it out, 'cause there's a lot of good memories in there… But that was my first experience of something like that and the t-shirt was a big part of it." Anon

There is a common narrative found throughout the world that dates from ancient religious beliefs, that to be materialistic, to possess an open affection for our 'stuff' is an indication of a shallow or superficial character. Heavy metal as a community negates this ethos[2] and the efficacy of Venom's work lies in the capacity for materials to absorb the experiences of the environment over time and bond a community together.

"To me band T-shirts are almost like a photo album of my life. Not just because some actually have dates on them, but they all remind me of a point in time… The points in time are most important – first gig, first gig at a particular venue, who I went with, who the support was, who my girlfriend was at the time, where I was working then, what I was driving at the time… Every T-shirt tells a story." Anon[3]

"One way to look at my art is that it is a collection of memories (from those that have donated material) sewn together in the form of a functional piece of artwork. Most metalheads will see a shirt or patch of a band they have seen live and immediately form a connection to the work." BV

As described by Venom himself, these artworks represent a collision of craft, fine art and the fringes of society. But they are fundamentally in and of themselves a collusion, a bringing together of different elements to create something entirely new without losing the soul of the originals. These fabrics possess a lived history and are knitted together to make a welcoming and inviting material. The inclusivity of these different elements within Venom's art also reflects an inherent inclusivity within metal, the only catch is an unconditional love of this melodious noise.

Lindsay Bishop

Doctoral Candidate, Department of Anthropology,
University College London

NOTES:

1   See 'Hellbent for Cooking: The Heavy Metal Cookbook' by Annick Giroux

2   As do many other cultures. See 'Handbook of Material Culture' ed Tilley et al for
    a more comprehensive anthropological perspective.

3   'Anon' quotations are from conversations with metalheads as part of my
    ongoing ethnographic research. 'BV' quotations are from Ben Venom.

Black Sabbath
AVFC
PREPARED

umbro
WEST HAM UNITED
LONDON
umbro
IRON MAIDEN
official

UP THE IRONS
IRON MAIDEN

right: *King Slayer,*
embroidery on LA Kings hockey jersey
27" x 35" (69 x 89cm), 2019

previous pages:
Up the Irons,
embroidery on West Ham United football shirt
22" x 29" (56 x 74cm), 2019

adidas
KINGS
SLAYER

King Slayer, (front view and detail)

KILLERS
Custom Fabricated Jacket
Collaboration with Jason Redwood,
Truth Never Told, and Lucien Shapiro
20" x 25" (51 x 63.5cm), 2019

Ben Venom

Ben Venom graduated from the San Francisco Art Institute in 2007 with a Master of Fine Arts degree. His work has been shown both nationally and internationally including the Levi Strauss Museum (Germany), National Folk Museum of Korea, HPGRP Gallery (Tokyo), Fort Wayne Museum, Charlotte Fogh Gallery (Denmark), Taubman Museum of Art, Gregg Museum of Art and Design, and the Craft and Folk Art Museum in Los Angeles. He has been interviewed by NPR: All Things Considered, Playboy, Juxtapoz Magazine, KQED, Maxim, and CBS Sunday Morning. Venom has lectured at the California College of Arts, the Frist Center for the Visual Arts, Midlands Arts Centre, Humboldt State University, Oregon College of Art and Craft, and Adidas. Recently, he was the artist in residence at MASS MoCA and the de Young Museum. Ben Venom is currently Visiting Faculty at the San Francisco Art Institute.

www.benvenom.com

Ben would like to thank: Kevin and Yvonne Taylor, Kevin King, Robert Graham, Brann Dailor, Truth Never Told, Jason Redwood, Lucien Shapiro, Kym Foglia, Randy Dodson, Midlands Arts Centre, Jess Litherland, Deborah Kermode, Silas Wood, Laura L Camerlengo, Lindsay Bishop, Home of Metal, Lisa Meyer and especially Megan and Beatrice Venom.

left: Ben Venom in his studio. Photo by Randy Dodson

HOME OF METAL

"I'm really proud to be a Brummie and to call Birmingham my home. Your surroundings and experiences influence your music so it's important for people to know where that music came from." **Tony Iommi, Black Sabbath**

HOME OF METAL is devoted to the music that was born in and around Birmingham, music that turned up the volume, down-tuned guitars, inspired generations of musicians and introduced a whole new meaning to the word 'heavy'. Home of Metal celebrates the forefathers of Heavy Metal, Black Sabbath, Judas Priest, Napalm Death and Godflesh throwing down the gauntlet to the city. Where are the shrines to Heavy Metal? Loved the world over, Heavy Metal in its many forms had its roots in Birmingham, but you wouldn't know to visit it. Nary a plaque, tour or tourist tea towel marked one of the city's most impactful cultural exports. But we're changing that.

Home of Metal joins the dots between music, social history, visual art and fan cultures to produce a new perspective on Heavy Metal. Through events and exhibitions Home of Metal celebrates the sound that originated in Birmingham, UK. Our work eschews notions of high and low art and instead bring audiences, artists and performers together to commemorate a unique sound and cultural heritage.

Our 2019 programme presents a series of exhibitions in partnership with organisations in and around Birmingham leading with Home of Metal: *Black Sabbath – 50 Years*, a major exhibition focused on Black Sabbath from the perspective of their fans, to show their impact and cultural legacy. The exhibition celebrates the diversity and loyalty of the bands global fanbase with over 3500+ portraits of fans captured from all corners of the world. With further lead exhibitions from artists: Ben Venom (US), Alan Kane (UK), Monster Chetwynd (UK), and Przemek Branas (Poland), that demonstrate Heavy Metal's reach into all corners of culture through explorations of fantasy, chaos, performance and fandom.

For more information **www.homeofmetal.com**

Home of Metal is created and produced by Capsule and is supported by Arts Council England, Heritage Lottery Fund, Laney Amplification and a range of project sponsors.

First published in 2019 by
Midlands Arts Centre
Cannon Hill Park
Birmingham B12 9QH
T: +44 (0)121 446 3232
www.macbirmingham.co.uk

Published on the occasion of the exhibition
ALL THIS MAYHEM, Ben Venom
Midlands Arts Centre
22 June–8 September 2019

This exhibition was produced in partnership with **Home of Metal**.
Home of Metal is a season that celebrates Birmingham's history of metal
music conceived and produced by Capsule. www.homeofmetal.com

© Midlands Arts Centre 2019
Texts copyright the authors, Laura L Camerlengo text edited by Danica Hodge.
Images copyright Ben Venom. Photography by Randy Dodson,
Monica Semergiu and Brandon Forrest Jensen.

Design by **aquarium graphic design ltd.**
07800 897886
aquariumgd@btinternet.com

Printed and bound by
Hill Shorter Limited,
54 Roebuck Lane,
West Bromwich,
West Midlands B70 6QP
Tel: +44 (0)121 553 7011
www.hillshorter.com

Distributed by
Cornerhouse Publications
HOME, 2 Tony Wilson Place
Manchester M15 4FN
Tel: +44 (0)161 2123466
publications@cornerhouse.org
www.cornerhousepublications.org

ISBN 978-1-907796-24-1

With support from the Roughley Trust